SOCCER SUP

STERLING

RULES

Hi, pleased to meet you.

We hope you enjoy our book about Raheem Sterling!

WELBECK

SIMON   DAN

THIS IS A WELBECK CHILDREN'S BOOK
Published in the USA in 2021 by Welbeck Children's Books Limited
An imprint of the Welbeck Publishing Group
20 Mortimer Street, London W1T 3JW
Text © 2020 Simon Mugford
Design & Illustration © 2020 Dan Green
ISBN: 978-1-78312-586-9

Writer: Simon Mugford
Designer and Illustrator: Dan Green
Design Manager: Sam James
Executive Editor: Suhel Ahmed
Production: Gary Hayes

Printed in the UK
10 9 8 7 6 5 4 3 2 1

Statistics and records correct as of February 2020

SOCCER SUPERSTARS

STERLING

RULES

SIMON MUGFORD   DAN GREEN

CONTENTS

CHAPTER 1

SUPER STERLING

5

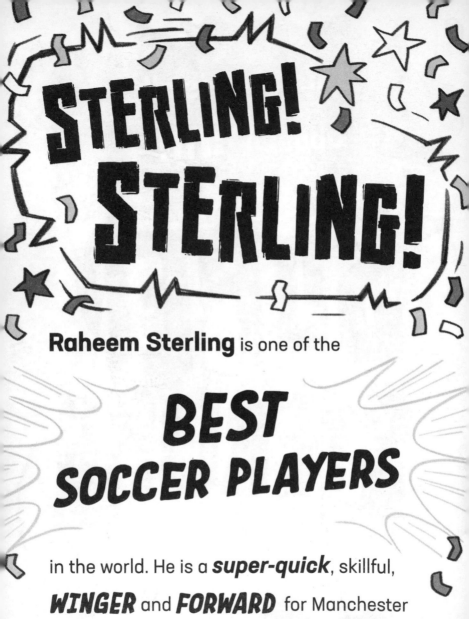

STERLING! STERLING!

Raheem Sterling is one of the

BEST SOCCER PLAYERS

in the world. He is a **super-quick**, skillful, **WINGER** and **FORWARD** for Manchester City and a key player for **ENGLAND.**

SO WHAT MAKES STERLING SO AWESOME?

Speed
One of the fastest players in the game.

Strength
Small, but strong enough to shake off defenders.

Creativity
Has clever ideas, moves, and tricks.

Flexibility
He can play on the wing, in midfield, or as a striker.

Goals and assists
Raheem scores and helps his teammates, too!

Sterling is simply one of the **best attacking players in the** WORLD!

9

CHECK OUT THE NUMBERS TO SEE HOW **GOOD** **STERLING** IS:

2 ...Premier League wins

1 ...FA Cup win

1 ...Golden Boy award

2 ...League Cup wins

1 ...FWA Footballer of the Year Award

STERLING I.D.

NAME: *Raheem Shaquille Sterling*

NICKNAME: *Raz*

DATE OF BIRTH: *December 8, 1994*

PLACE OF BIRTH: *Kingston, Jamaica*

HEIGHT: *5 ft. 7 in. (1.7 m)*

POSITION: *Winger / forward*

CLUBS: *Liverpool, Manchester City*

NATIONAL TEAM: *England*

LEFT- OR RIGHT-FOOTED: *Right*

CHAPTER 2

STARTING OUT

Raheem Sterling was born in **Jamaica** in **1994.** He lived there with his mom, grandmother, and his sisters Kimberley and Lakima.

JAMAICA

KINGSTON

14

Raheem and his family **loved each other** very, very much. But the other thing Raheem loved was . . .

SOCCER!

Life was tough in Jamaica, so when Raheem was **five,** he moved with his mom and sisters—to **England!**

ENGLAND

They lived in northwest London.

JAMAICA

Raheem found it hard to **settle down** at first. He was a bit **naughty** and got into **trouble at school.**

HIS MOM WORRIED ABOUT HIM.

But Raheem **LOVED SOCCER.**
Playing soccer **kept him out of trouble,** so Raheem's mom loved soccer, too!

A local social worker and soccer coach called **Clive Ellington** spotted Raheem playing with his friends.

Clive asked Raheem to join the local youth team, *ALPHA AND OMEGA.*

Raheem quickly became Alpha and Omega's

STAR PLAYER.

Raheem was small, fast, and **much, MUCH** better than anyone else. The bigger boys couldn't cope with his **skills and tricks,** so they would **foul** him.

OUCH!

Raheem would sometimes get into **trouble** with the **referee,** especially if his side was losing. He always wanted to **win.**

But **Clive** helped him **focus** on his game and Raheem got **better and better.**

Copland Community School had one of the **best** soccer teams in **London.** When Raheem joined the school at 11, they got **even better!**

HE WAS THE **TEAM CAPTAIN** AND HELPED THEM WIN LOTS OF **TROPHIES!**

Raheem grew up near **Wembley,** close to where the new **stadium** was being built.

As a boy, he **DREAMED** of playing there one day.

AND OF COURSE, HE WOULD!

"HE NEVER REALIZED HOW GOOD HE WAS —HE JUST LOVED SOCCER."

Clive Ellington

28

CHAPTER 3

QPR STAR

When Raheem was 10, he joined the academy at a club in west London:

QUEEN'S PARK RANGERS

At **QPR,** they soon saw that although Raheem was **small**, he was **tough!** He was **too good** for the **under-12s,** so when he was **11** he played for the **under-14s.**

He played for the

under-16s

when he

was **13** . . .

. . . **and Raheem** was still the **BEST**

player by far. **Nobody** could **stop** him.

Raheem still played for his school team, too!

At **14,** Raheem was playing in the QPR **under-18s.** He even trained with the **first team.**

YOU'RE A **NATURAL,** RAHEEM!

34

Scouts from top clubs like **Arsenal, Chelsea, Manchester City,** and **Tottenham** came to watch him play.

At the same time, some of Raheem's friends were getting in trouble at school. Raheem wanted to stay **out of trouble**, so it was time to move on.

BUT WHERE TO?

CHAPTER 4

RED RAHEEM

In **2010,** when he was **15 years old,** Raheem signed for one of the most famous teams in the world:

LIVERPOOL

40

The Liverpool manager **Rafa Benítez** signed him for

$650,000.

Liverpool had a fantastic **history** and some **awesome** players, like:

Jamie Carragher

in defense . . .

Steven Gerrard

in midfield . . .

and star striker

Fernando Torres.

Knock, knock.

Who's there?

General Lee.

General Lee who?

General Lee I support Ipswich Town, but I like Liverpool, too!

Raheem soon made a name for himself in the **Liverpool youth** teams. In an **FA Youth Cup** game against **Southend United** in February 2011, Raheem scored an amazing **FIVE** goals as they won **9-0.**

BOOM!

Caretaker manager **Kenny Dalglish** gave Raheem his **Premier League** debut in **March 2012**. He came on as a **substitute** in the 84th minute against **Wigan**.

Kenny Dalglish

IT WAS JUST THE BEGINNING!

Raheem was 17 years, 107 days old on his *Premier League* debut.

47

New manager **Brendan Rodgers** started Raheem against **Manchester City** in the second league game of the **2012-13** season.

RAHEEM WAS AWESOME! Defenders were afraid of his **speed and skills**.

He scored his first Liverpool goal against **Reading** in the **Premier League** in **October 2012.** At the time, he was Liverpool's *SECOND-YOUNGEST* goalscorer.

49

"WHAT I LOVED ABOUT RAHEEM WAS THAT, FOR A YOUNG BOY . . . HE KNEW WHAT HE WANTED TO BE . . . HE WANTED TO BE ONE OF THE BEST PLAYERS IN THE WORLD."

Brendan Rodgers

CHAPTER 5

COOL KID

PREMIER LEAGUE 2013-14

HIGHLIGHTS FROM A BIG SEASON IN THE PREMIERSHIP FOR RAHEEM.

DECEMBER 4, 2013

LIVERPOOL 5-1 NORWICH CITY

Raheem provided an assist for one of Luis Suárez's **FOUR** goals, then Suárez returned the favor to set up Sterling's first goal of the season.

FEBRUARY 8, 2014

LIVERPOOL 5-1 ARSENAL

*Arsenal may have been top of the league but were no match for the Reds as Sterling scored **TWO** of their five goals—his first **brace** for Liverpool.*

APRIL 20, 2014

NORWICH CITY 2-3 LIVERPOOL

*Raheem was involved in all three of Liverpool's goals—scoring **TWO** and assisting Suárez as Norwich were beaten again.*

BOOM!

In **2013-14,** Sterling, with forwards **Luis Suárez** and **Daniel Sturridge** made an awesome attacking trio.

STERLING'S 2013-14 RECORD

APPEARANCES	GOALS	ASSISTS
38	10	9

Raheem was on the **shortlist** of the PFA Young Player of the Year Award and was voted Liverpool's **Young Player of the Year.**

He was still only *19!*

57

2014-15

**HIGHLIGHTS
OF STERLING'S
LAST SEASON
AT LIVERPOOL.**

AUGUST 17, 2014

LIVERPOOL 2-1 SOUTHAMPTON

Sterling got Liverpool's season off to a flying start as he scored one goal and assisted with the other in this home win over Southampton.

AUGUST 31, 2014

TOTTENHAM 0-3 LIVERPOOL

Raheem's pace and skill brought another opening goal as Spurs were beaten at home. Sterling was Man of the Match.

Raheem played his
100th game for Liverpool
in December 2014—against Manchester United.

In the **2014-15** season, Sterling played in
seven different positions for Liverpool:

CENTER-FORWARD

SECOND STRIKER

LEFT WING

ATTACKING MIDFIELD

RIGHT WING

LEFT MIDFIELD

RIGHT MIDFIELD

LEFT-BACK

CENTER-BACK

CENTER-BACK

RIGHT-BACK

GOALKEEPER

In **December 2014,** shortly after he turned **20,** Raheem won the Golden Boy award for the **best player in Europe** age 21 or younger.

GREAT GOAL

JANUARY 20, 2015

LEAGUE CUP SEMIFINAL, FIRST LEG

LIVERPOOL 1-1 CHELSEA

The Reds were trailing 1-0 from an **Eden Hazard** penalty, when Sterling picked up the ball and ran straight at the Chelsea defense!

FWAP!

He flew past **Nemanja Matić** and
Gary Cahill and *BAM!*

STERLING'S LIVERPOOL RECORD

APPEARANCES	GOALS	ASSISTS
129	23	25

CHAPTER 6

STERLING STYLES

Scoring a goal means it's time for a

CELEBRATION!

Sterling has a few . . .

The **W** over his face is a Jamaican sign.

Leaping high

in the air.

Pointing to the sky, just

like **Lionel Messi** does!

TOP CUTS

Dreadlocks?

Raheem's had a few different hairstyles. **Which one is your favorite?**

Flattop?

68

Sterling is a global celebrity sports star with *ICE COOL STYLE.* He's appeared in:

SPORTSWEAR ADS

A VIDEO WITH RAP STARS DAVE AND STORMZY.

Dave

STORMZY

Raheem has used his profile to support charities, community groups, and families affected by London's Grenfell Tower fire.

CHAPTER 7

CITY BOY

In the summer of **2015,** Raheem signed for

MANCHESTER CITY!

The deal was worth an estimated **$60 MILLION.** He was given the **number 7 shirt.**

He was the most expensive English player ever!

PREMIER LEAGUE 2015-16

HIGHLIGHTS OF STERLING'S FIRST PREMIER LEAGUE SEASON WITH CITY.

AUGUST 10, 2015

WEST BROM 0-3 MANCHESTER CITY

Raheem went straight into the line-up for City's opening game of the season.

A great away win!

AUGUST 29, 2015

MANCHESTER CITY 2-0 WATFORD

*Raheem scored his **first** Manchester City goal in the 47th minute of this home win over Watford.*

OCTOBER 17, 2015

MANCHESTER CITY 5-1 BOURNEMOUTH

*Sterling was playing in a central position as a second striker and—**BOOM!** He scored his first ever **hat trick**.*

77

LEAGUE CUP WINNER

SEPTEMBER 22, 2015

LEAGUE CUP THIRD ROUND

SUNDERLAND 1-4 MANCHESTER CITY

Sterling set City on their way in the **League Cup** with a ***GOAL*** and two assists.

FEBRUARY 28, 2016

LEAGUE CUP FINAL, WEMBLEY

LIVERPOOL 1-1 MANCHESTER CITY

(CITY WON 3-1 ON PENALTIES)

In the final, Sterling and City **beat** his old club, in his old neighborhood to win his *FIRST TROPHY!*

Pep Guardiola was the new manager.

CHAMPIONS LEAGUE GOALS

NOVEMBER 3, 2015

CHAMPIONS LEAGUE GROUP STAGE

SEVILLA 1-3 MANCHESTER CITY

Raheem opened the scoring for City with an 8th-minute goal in this away win in Spain.

This was his first ever goal in the Champions League.

DECEMBER 8, 2015

CHAMPIONS LEAGUE GROUP STAGE

MANCHESTER CITY 4-2
BORUSSIA MÖNCHENGLADBACH

Sterling put in an awesome performance against the German side, providing an **assist** and scoring *TWO* late goals.

STERLING'S 2015–16 RECORD

APPEARANCES	GOALS	ASSISTS
47	11	10

82

CHAPTER 8

HEROES AND RIVALS

As a boy, Raheem had his favorite players—**just like you do!** He loved **FAST, ATTACKING PLAYERS** with lots of **CLEVER SKILLS** and **TRICKS.**

He was a big fan of the **Brazilian** star **RONALDINHO.**

RAHEEM IS ONE OF THE BEST FORWARDS IN THE LEAGUE.

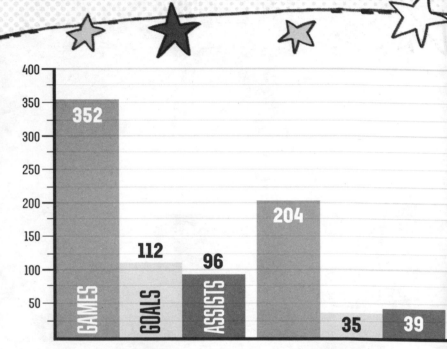

352 — GAMES
112 — GOALS
96 — ASSISTS
204
35
39

RAHEEM STERLING
LIVERPOOL / MANCHESTER CITY

WILFRIED ZAHA
*MANCHESTER UTD / CARDIFF CITY
/ CRYSTAL PALACE*

COMPARE HIS **ALL-TIME PREMIER LEAGUE** STATS WITH SOME RIVALS:

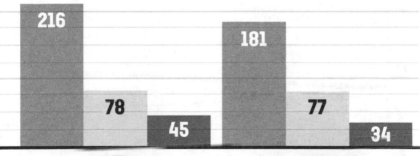

216

78

45

181

77

34

SON HEUNG-MIN
TOTTENHAM HOTSPUR

SADIO MANÉ
SOUTHAMPTON / LIVERPOOL

WORLD FORWARDS

Some of the most valuable forwards in the world in **2020:**

RAHEEM STERLING

CLUB: **MANCHESTER CITY**

COUNTRY: **ENGLAND**

EST VALUE: **$150 MILLION**

NEYMAR

CLUB: **PARIS SAINT-GERMAIN**

COUNTRY: **BRAZIL**

EST VALUE: **$150 MILLION**

JADON SANCHO

CLUB: *BORUSSIA DORTMUND*

COUNTRY: *ENGLAND*

EST VALUE: *$136 MILLION*

EDEN HAZARD

CLUB: *REAL MADRID*

COUNTRY: *BELGIUM*

EST VALUE: *$140 MILLION*

THEY'RE ALL GOOD ON THE WING, LIKE ME!

ALAN ALBATROSS
TOP WINGER

LEGENDS ON THE WINGS

Like **Raheem,** these legendary wingers from the past had **skill, speed,** and **creativity.**

JOHN BARNES 1980-99

Born in Jamaica, Barnes was a legend for Watford, Liverpool, and England. He won two league championships and two FA Cups.

DAVID BECKHAM 1992-2013

The Manchester United and Real Madrid midfield master won six Premier League titles, the FA Cup, the Champions League, and La Liga.

RYAN GIGGS 1990-2014

With over 900 games for Manchester United, the Welsh wing wizard won 13 Premier League titles, four FA Cups, and the Champions League twice.

ROBERT PIRES
1993-2015

Alongside Thierry Henry, Pires helped a great Arsenal side win two Premier League titles and three FA Cups.

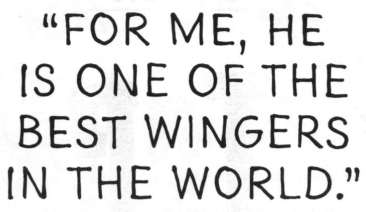

CHAPTER 8

TOP CLASS

2016-17

HIGHLIGHTS OF STERLING'S SECOND SEASON WITH CITY.

AUGUST 28, 2016

PREMIER LEAGUE

MANCHESTER CITY 3-1 WEST HAM

*Raheem got on the scorecard with **TWO** goals in this early-season home win.*

He was voted Premier League Player of the Month in August.

FEBRUARY 21, 2017

CHAMPIONS LEAGUE ROUND OF 16

MANCHESTER CITY 5-3 MONACO

*Sterling **scored** and provided an **assist** for **Sergio Agüero** in this epic Champions League game.*

STERLING'S
2016-17 RECORD

APPEARANCES	GOALS	ASSISTS
47	10	20

2017-18

In **Pep Guardiola's** second full season as manager, Raheem got **better and better** as a player.

He scored **FOUR** goals in the **Champions League** and **18** in the **Premier League**, including some important **late** winners.

RECORD BREAKERS!

Raheem won the **Premier League** in a **record-breaking** season.

MANCHESTER CITY RECORDED...

...the most points in the Premier League:

100

. . . the most wins:  **32**

. . . the most goals:  **106**

. . . and the best

goal difference:  **+79**

KEEPING SCORE

BY ADAM UPP

"HE WILL BE A TOP, TOP PLAYER BECAUSE HE'S SO FAST, A DYNAMIC PLAYER, AND HAS CHARACTER ONE-ON-ONE. HE IS AN EXCELLENT GUY . . ."

Pep Guardiola

100

YOUNG LION

Raheem has been an **England player** since appearing for the **under-16s.** In **2011,** he played at the **Under-17 World Cup** in **Mexico,** where he scored against **Rwanda** and **Argentina.**

Raheem is a key player for England. He took part in the **2014 World Cup, EURO 2016,** and the **2018 World Cup,** where the team reached the

semifinal for

the first time in

28 YEARS.

NATIONS LEAGUE STAR

OCTOBER 15, 2018

NATIONS LEAGUE GROUP STAGE, SEVILLE

SPAIN 2-3 ENGLAND

Sterling had not scored for England in **27 GAMES.** He was determined to change that—*AND HE DID!*

In the **15th minute** of the game, he picked up a pass from **Marcus Rashford** and *BANG!* He scored a fantastic *GOAL!*

Rashford scored,

then shortly before

halftime, **Sterling**

had the ball in

the back of the

net *AGAIN!*

THWACK!

GOoAAALLL!

ENGLAND WERE AWESOME AND **STERLING** WAS **MAN OF THE MATCH.**

This was England's first win in Spain since *1987.*

HAT TRICK HERO

MARCH 22, 2019

EURO 2020 QUALIFIER, WEMBLEY

ENGLAND 5-0 CZECH REPUBLIC

This was the first match in England's qualifying campaign for **EURO 2020.**

RAHEEM WAS ON FIRE!

His pace was too much for the **Czechs** and he opened the scoring in the **24th minute.** Then he won a penalty, which **Harry Kane** scored, before netting *TWO* more goals in the second half.

BOOM!

Raheem scored his **first England hat trick** under the **Wembley arch**—just like he'd dreamed about as a boy.

"HE HAS HAD DIFFICULT MOMENTS —BUT HE'S TURNED FULL CIRCLE. I'M DELIGHTED FOR HIM."

England manager Gareth Southgate

108

CHAPTER 11

TREBLE TIME

PREMIER LEAGUE 2018-19

HIGHLIGHTS OF A MASSIVE SEASON FOR RAHEEM AND CITY.

NOVEMBER 4, 2018

MANCHESTER CITY 6-1 SOUTHAMPTON

Raheem fired home **TWO** goals and assisted two more as Southampton were thrashed.

FEBRUARY 10, 2019

MANCHESTER CITY 6-0 CHELSEA

Another **TWO** goals from Raheem, along with a **Sergio Agüero hat trick**, saw the Londoners soundly beaten.

MARCH 9, 2019

MANCHESTER CITY 3-1 WATFORD

Raheem scored **THREE GOALS** inside **14 minutes** to win the game for City.

CUP KINGS

Raheem won his second **League Cup** medal when City won the competition in **February 2019.**

The final, against **Chelsea,** went to penalties and **Sterling scored** the winning shoot-out kick.

Then in May, **Sterling** starred again as **Watford** were beaten **6-0** in the **FA Cup Final.** His **two goals** and an assist helped City win their **second cup competition** of the season.

CHAMPIONS

(AGAIN!)

The battle for the **Premier League** title went right to the last day of the season. City beat **Brighton and Hove Albion** **4-1** to win the title with **98 points.**

Raheem's **17 goals** helped City win the title for a second season in a row and complete their first ever

TREBLE!

"I'M JUST DELIGHTED. THIS IS EXACTLY WHAT I CAME TO THE CLUB FOR, TO WIN TROPHIES AND BE IN THESE MOMENTS."

Raheem Sterling, on winning the treble with Manchester City.

116

CHAPTER 12

STAR QUALITY

ROLE MODEL

Raheem has come a long, long way from the **naughty student** playing soccer on a London street. Now he's one of the ***WORLD'S BEST PLAYERS*** — and more.

Sterling has spoken out against ***RACISM*** in ***SOCCER*** and elsewhere. He still **dazzles** on the field and is now a **global star** and a **role model** for millions.

Raheem got the **2019-20** season off to an incredible start, scoring a **hat trick** in City's opening game against **West Ham**.

He also scored his first Champions League hat trick— against Atalanta in October.

STERLING'S MANCHESTER CITY RECORD IN ALL COMPETITIONS:

SEASON	APPS	GOALS	ASSISTS
2015-16	47	11	10
2016-17	47	10	20
2017-18	46	23	17
2018-19	51	25	18
2019-20	36	20	7

HONORS AND AWARDS

PREMIER LEAGUE WINNER
2017–18
2018–19

FA CUP WINNER
2018–19

LEAGUE CUP WINNER
2015–16
2018–19

FA COMMUNITY SHIELD
2019

GOLDEN BOY AWARD
2014

QUIZ TIME!

How much do you know about **Raheem Sterling?** Try this quiz to find out, then test your friends!

1. Which London team did Raheem join as a youth player?

----

2. Which stadium did Raheem live near as a boy?

----

3. How much did Liverpool sign Sterling for in 2010?

----

4. How many goals did Sterling score for Liverpool?

----

5. Which shirt number does Raheem wear at Manchester City?

---

6. In which season did Raheem win his first Premier League title?

---

7. Against which team did Raheem score a hat trick for England in 2019?

---

8. Which team did Manchester City beat 6-0 to win the FA Cup in 2019?

---

9. Where was Raheem born?

---

10. How many goals did Sterling score for Manchester City in 2018-19?

The answers are on the next page *but no peeking!*

ANSWERS

1. Queen's Park Rangers
2. Wembley
3. $650,000
4. 23
5. Number 7
6. 2017-18
7. Czech Republic
8. Watford
9. Jamaica
10. 25